GW00391836

FERRIES
of the
ENGLISH
CHANNEL
Past and
Present

Published by

FERRY
Publications Ltd

ISBN: 1 871947 43X

PO Box 9, Narberth, Pembrokeshire, SA68 0SA. Tel: +44(0) 1834 891460 Fax: +44 (0) 1834 891463

Introduction

Volume 1 of this publication was produced in December 1992, prior to the opening of the Channel Tunnel and its ramifications. The tunnel opened in 1995, and immediately was an attraction to many travellers on the channel routes but as we draw to the end of the decade, traffic is beginning to go back to the ferries. The fire in the "fixed link" in 1996 saw an immediate return of passengers, cars and freight to the ferries, and since its re-opening to traffic, the tunnel has struggled to get back to its pre-fire levels. By October 1997, between P&O European Ferries, Stena Line, SeaFrance and Hoverspeed on the Dover Strait operations, the share of passenger and freight traffic attracted by the ferries currently stood at around 85% against Eurotunnel at 15%. The western sector of the English Channel operated by Brittany Ferries and P&O European Ferries during 1997 were also to see an increase of traffic returning after the honeymoon period of the tunnel for the last three years.

As a result of the tunnel's opening, the ferry companies have had a period of consolidation, with very little expansion or new-building. The last five years have also seen some long-established routes disappearing, possibly the greatest loss was the demise of RMT in February 1997. Ferry companies have also come and gone, like Eurolink, who tried to replace the luxurious service of Olau with "second-rate" tonnage from Greece. The early success of BCIF saw the demise of the company in 1994, when they failed to replace the *Rozel* with suitable tonnage for the Channel Island services.

Since the last edition of the title, only one purpose-built vessel has been constructed for the Continental operations, the *Pride of Burgundy*. Modifications have been undertaken to tonnage to increase their capacity or suitability for their new role, like

Title page: The *Val de Loire* arrives at Santander after her 23 hour passage from Plymouth. *(Miles Cowsill)*
Above: The *Stena Antrim* and the *Stena Lynx III* seen at Newhaven in June 1997. *(John May)*

Above: The 17 year old *SeaFrance Renoir* arrives at Calais in September 1997. SeaFrance have become the second principal operator on the Dover-Calais service since dissolving their partnership with Stena Line in 1995. *(Miles Cowsill)*

Below: The *SuperSeaCat Two* was introduced on the Dover-Calais service by Hoverspeed in June 1997. After only one season on the English Channel, the Italian-built craft is due to transfer to the Irish Sea in March 1998 to the Liverpool-Dublin route. *(Sea Containers)*

the *Stena Empereur*, *Val de Loire* and *Pride of Bilbao*, which have all been transferred from the Baltic during the last five years.

Fast ferries have become more prominent on the Channel in the last five years. Not all have been successful, like the *Stena Pegasus*. It is rather ironic to think that the sixties-built SRN4 hovercraft have just continued to operate successfully as originally, at the grand age of 35 years old. Hoverspeed still claim they are the quickest way across the channel with a crossing time of 35 minutes between Dover and Calais.

The planned ending of the duty-free arrangement in June 1999 is also concentrating minds, with a loss of revenue and the inevitable increase in fares which will follow. In the light of this loss of revenue and the tunnel, it has forced the ferry companies to introduce radical changes in their operations, including a joint venture agreement between Stena Line and P&O European Ferries, which would have been totally unthinkable five years' ago. As we went to press, the merger had been agreed upon by the government; it will see a reduction of ferries on the Dover-Calais service during 1998 to a fleet of around 14 ships, compared to 1997 of 16 ferries. This merger is likely to open the gates further joint ventures or mergers as competition for a share of the market increases on other routes on the English Channel.

During the last 12 months, Stena Line have seen a rapid decline in their operations on the Dover Strait, while their future operating partners P&O European Ferries have seen their profits rise dramatically with their very superior service. The once-third operator between Dover and Calais, SeaFrance, formerly SNAT/SNCF, have become the second key operator on the shortest route between Britain and France in the last two years, putting their former partners Stena Line into third position.

Sally Holyman Ferries took over the historic Ostend service on 1st March, their fortunes to date at Ramsgate have been mixed, and as we went to press the company were considering the transfer of their operations to Dover and a possible joint marketing campaign with Hoverspeed, instead of Sally. Meanwhile the freight operation of Sally Ferries, however, has been blessed with improved fortunes in recent months.

The attractive Newhaven-Dieppe service still very much is a day-trip operation, June 1999 may possibly see a further decline in its fortunes and its possible closure. Operations for Brittany Ferries and P&O European Ferries have been extremely difficult for both operators since the opening of the fixed link, however there appears to be light at the end of the tunnel for both of them, with very encouraging signs in trade returning to both operators on the western channel and continued demand on their Spanish operations.

The Channel Islands saw the demise of BCIF in 1994 and the expansion of Condor's operations to the UK with their fast craft operations, which have been plagued with difficulties, inevitably leading to calls from the islanders for investment in a conventional ferry to operate in tandem with the InCat craft.

Travellers to the Isle of Wight have seen improvement in tonnage in the last five years by Red Funnel, their competitors Wightlink meanwhile have continued to consolidate their share of the market.

Above: Originally planned to be built for the Dover-Zeebrugge service as the **European Causeway**, the vessel was later completed as a passenger vessel for the Dover-Calais service to meet capacity demands on the link. She is seen here arriving at Dover named the **Pride of Burgundy** for the first time in 1993. *(FotoFlite)*

In this second edition, the book is slightly laid out differently. The first chapter includes photographs of the current ships operating from the European mainland from Zeebrugge to Santander to the shores of Britain, including the Isle of Wight. The next chapter of the publication includes a varied selection of photographs of companies which have come and gone in the nineties and also ships that have disappeared with their age or are operating under a new guise today. The final part of the title includes a selection of photographs of the RMT fleet over the last 25 years which includes pictures of all the different liveries of company which have used since the sixties. I am indebted to my business partner, John Hendy, for his guidance with the book and to John May, John Bryant, Dave Hocquard, Matthew Punter, Mike Louagie, and our good friends at FotoFlite for their assistance with this book.

I hope that you will enjoy this title, which will be joined in 1998 by its counterpart on the vessels of the Irish Sea.

Miles Cowsill

Above: Dart Line operates three Rumanian vessels on their links from Dartford to Zeebrugge and Vlissingen. The **Dart 2** is seen here with her sister the **Dart 4** off the Kent coast. *(FotoFlite)*

Below: Cobelfret are a Belgium-based company providing freight links between Zeebrugge and Purfleet and Zeebrugge and Immingham. The company currently operate ten vessels, two of them are seen here at Zeebrugge in October 1997 on their Sunday layover; with one of the Fred Olsen freight ships which also operate from the port to Norway, Germany and Britain. *(Miles Cowsill)*

Above: The Felixstowe passenger service was opened in 1972 by the *Viking II*. It subsequently closed to passengers some 21 years later. Today the route is maintained as a freight-only service with the chartered German vessels *Thomas Wehr* and *Gabriele Wehr*.(pictured here) outward-bound at the entrance to the Orwell estuary. This view also takes in the *Prince of Scandinavia* inward-bound from Hamburg. *(FotoFlite)*

Below: With the introduction of the *European Highway, European Pathway* (pictured here) and *European Seaway* in the early nineties by P&O on their Dover-Zeebrugge route, the company have continued to consolidate the operation established by Townsend Car Ferries in 1965, despite the fixed link. *(Miles Cowsill)*

Above: Following the traditional ferry service from Ostend to Ramsgate being closed by RMT in February 1997, two InCat craft, the **Holyman Diamant** and the **Holyman Rapide** were introduced on the new 100 minute service by Holyman Sally Ferries. The two Australian-built craft with capacity for 700 passengers and 180 cars operate in tandem with the traditional ferry **Eurotraveller** (ex. **Sally Sky**) which is seen here outward-bound to Ostend with the **Holyman Rapide**. *(FotoFlite)*

Below: Built as the **Argo**, this vessel has been much travelled in European waters, including charters with North Sea Ferries, Olau Line, P&O European Ferries, TT Line and Dart Line, to name a few. Today, renamed the **Euroway**, she maintains the Ramsgate-Ostend freight service, as probably one of the most attractive-looking freight ships on the English Channel. *(FotoFlite)*

Above: Built for the Holyman Group as *Condor 12* for the Channel Islands service; in 1997 she was renamed *Holyman Rapide* for her new role on the Ramsgate-Ostend route. The 81 metre InCat craft is seen here departing from Ramsgate in October 1997. *(Miles Cowsill)*

Below: The *Condor 10* was built in 1993 and is seen here at the end of the now defunct Ramsgate-Dunkerque route. This craft during her four year career has seen service not only on the Channel Islands route but also in the Baltic, the Irish Sea and winter operations in New Zealand. In 1998 she is due to operate a new route for Condor Ferries between Weymouth, St. Peter Port and St. Malo. *(Miles Cowsill)*

Above: The Croatian-registered *Eurocruiser* (ex *Rosebay*) is seen here leaving Ostend for Ramsgate. This vessel until March 1997 was employed on the Harwich-Hook of Holland service for Stena Line BV. *(Miles Cowsill)*

Below: This late evening view takes in the *Pride of Kent* outward-bound for Calais and the former train ferry *SeaFrance Nord Pas-de-Calais*. The train ferry service which the *SeaFrance Nord Pas-de-Calais* was built for closed in December 1995. *(Miles Cowsill)*

Above and Below: This view shows the *Pride of Kent* (ex. *Spirit of Free Enterprise*) arriving at Calais prior to her jumboisation during the winter of 1991/92. It is interesting to compare the vessel's current profile in the picture below of her outward-bound from Calais off Cap Gris-Naz. *(Mike Louagie/Miles Cowsill)*

Above: The *Pride of Dover* and *Pride of Calais* (pictured here) were purpose-built for the Dover-Calais service. The success of this route is primarily due to these two purpose-built vessels. *(Mike Louagie)*

Below: Built as the *St. Anselm* for the Dover-Calais service by Sealink in 1980, the *Stena Cambria* returned to her former route in 1996 after four years on the Irish Sea. The 'Cambria' is seen here swinging in the Eastern Docks at Dover after layover during the night for engine repairs. *(Miles Cowsill)*

Above: The *Pride of Bruges* goes astern from the port of Calais in October 1997. Originally built by Townsend Thoresen as the *Pride of Free Enterprise*, she was later renamed *Pride of Bruges* and transferred to the Dover-Zeebrugge passenger service. The vessel has become too small for the Calais route and will probably be transferred to the Newhaven-Dieppe route in 1998. *(Miles Cowsill)*

Below: The *Stena Empereur* was transferred to the Dover-Calais route in 1996 in an effort to offer additional capacity for the Company. The vessel was originally built as the *Stena Jutlandica* for the Gothenburg-Frederikshavn service in 1983. She currently is the largest ferry on the Dover Strait. *(FotoFlite)*

Above: The *Stena Invicta* was built originally for DSB (Danish State Railways) as the *Peder Paars*. In 1990 she was purchased by Stena Line for the Dover-Calais route. She is due to be withdrawn from operations in 1998 under the new P&O Stena Line agreement *(Miles Cowsill)*

Below: Not viewed from her best angle, the *Pride of Burgundy* is seen here swinging off the berth at Calais. The vessel has a capacity for 1,420 passengers and 600 cars. *(Miles Cowsill)*

Above & Below: The *SeaFrance Cezanne* (ex. *Fiesta*) was converted in Germany during the winter of 1989/90 for SNAT, with the 'Fantasia' (pictured below as the *Stena Fantasia*) in a joint arrangement with Sealink and SNAT to increase capacity on the route for the two companies following the introduction of P&O's new vessels. *(Miles Cowsill)*

Above: The *SeaFrance Renoir* (ex. *Cote D'Azur*) has been employed on the Calais-Dover service since she was originally built in 1981. Additional superstructure at the stern was added to the vessel in 1996 when all the fleet received a major overhaul following the demise of their joint agreement with Stena Line the previous year. *(Miles Cowsill)*

Below: The *SeaFrance Monet* seen here arriving at Calais from Dover on her one-and-only season in August 1996. Originally built as the *Stena Danica*, subsequently renamed *Stena Nordica* and later *Stena Nautica*, she has seen service for RMT on the Ostend-Dover route and later as the *Versailles* on the Dieppe-Newhaven link for SNCF. In 1992 she was renamed the *Stena Londoner* for the relaunch of the Newhaven-Dieppe route by Stena Sealink Line. *(Miles Cowsill)*

Above: The *SeaFrance Manet* was originally built as the SNCF as the *Champs Elysees* for the Calais/Boulogne-Dover route in 1984. In 1990 she was transferred to the Dieppe-Newhaven service and later chartered by Stena Sealink when they took over the operation. She was subsequently named the *Stena Parisien* and on the completion of her charter to the Swedish company she returned to SeaFrance in 1997, displacing the *SeaFrance Monet* on the Calais route. *(Miles Cowsill)*

Below: The *SuperSeaCat Two* was launched at the Italian yard of Fincantieri on 22nd March 1997. This impressive picture shows the vessel being rolled out of the builder's hanger. The *SuperSeaCat Two* entered commercial operations on the Dover-Calais route on 23rd June 1997. *(Fincantieri)*

Above: The *Hoverspeed Great Britain* was originally launched as the *Christopher Columbus* but was renamed prior to winning the Hales Trophy for "Blue Riband of the Atlantic". In 1990 she inaugurated the unsuccessful fast ferry service between Portsmouth and Cherbourg. Today she maintains the only ferry link between Folkestone and Boulogne. The 74 metre craft is seen here leaving Boulogne. *(Miles Cowsill)*

Below: Despite all the changes on the Dover Strait during the last thirty years, the hovercraft operations of Hoverspeed have continued successfully. This view shows the stretched hovercraft, *The Princess Anne*, leaving the Western Docks at Dover for Calais. The hovercraft operation still is the fastest way across the channel even with the opening of the Channel Tunnel. *(Miles Cowsill)*

Above: Hoverspeed Falcon Seafreight, is a joint venture between Sea Containers and Falcon Distribution (UK), they operate the *Picasso* on their Folkestone-Boulogne service. This 20 year old vessel originally built as the *Wuppertal* maintains normally three round sailings a day between the two ports. *(FotoFlite)*
Below: The *Stena Antrim* (ex. *St. Christopher*) seen arriving at Newhaven in July 1997 from Dieppe. The 'Antrim' is due to be displaced from the Newhaven-Dieppe service in 1998 and replaced by the *Pride of Bruges*. *(John May)*

Above: The *Stena Lynx III* chartered by Stena Line in 1996 for the Dover-Calais service was transferred to the Newhaven-Dieppe route in 1997, following the unsuccessful operation of *Stena Pegasus*. *(FotoFlite)*

Below: The *Duc de Normandie* has maintained the Caen-Portsmouth service for Brittany Ferries for the last 11 years. Originally built as the *Prinses Beatrix* for SMZ she still maintains very much her original profile. The vessel underwent an extensive refit in 1997. *(FotoFlite)*

Above: This stern view shows the *Normandie* leaving Portsmouth for Caen in April 1996. The Finnish-built vessel set new standards of operations on the English Channel on entering service in 1992. *(Miles Cowsill)*

Below: In 1993 the *Pride of Bilbao* was chartered by P&O European Ferries to inaugurate their new Portsmouth-Bilbao service. During most of the year she operates two round trips to Spain a week plus one round trip between Portsmouth and Cherbourg. Built for Viking Line in 1986 as the *Olympia*, she is currently the largest ferry operating out of UK waters. She is seen here arriving at Portsmouth. *(Miles Cowsill)*

This impressive view of part of the naval dockyard at Portsmouth takes in the **Pride of Portsmouth** arriving from Le Havre and Nelson's flagship, the HMS **Victory**. The **Pride of Portsmouth** and **Pride of Le Havre** were chartered by P&O European Ferries in 1994 following the demise of Olau Line.

(P&O European Ferries)

Above: Built as the *Viking Valiant* for the Southampton-Le Havre service in 1975, the *Pride of Cherbourg* is seen here leaving Portsmouth following her jumboisation in 1986. The *Pride of Cherbourg* and her sister the *Pride of Hampshire* have maintained the Cherbourg link together since 1994. *(Miles Cowsill)*

Below: The much-travelled *Purbeck* is seen here arriving at Ouistreham whilst on charter to Brittany Ferries. Originally built for Truckline Ferries for their Cherbourg-Poole service in 1978, the vessel has seen service for numerous companies since her displacement from the Brittany Ferries' fleet in 1994. The *Purbeck* has been chartered by BCIF, Commodore Ferries, Sally Line, Dart Line and Irish Ferries during the last three years and currently is chartered by Gaelic Ferries to operate between Cork and Cherbourg. *(Miles Cowsill)*

Above: Irish Ferries' *Saint Killian II* seen at Le Havre in 1997 prior to her departure for Rosslare. The vessel completed her last sailing for the company in September 1997 as she no longer complies with the latest SOLAS requirements. The 'Killian' will be replaced in 1998 by the former *Stena Normandy* - see page 42. *(Miles Cowsill)*

Below: The *Barfleur* is seen here outward-bound from Poole for Cherbourg. In 1997 the *Barfleur* made her inaugural sailing to Spain, when she deputised for the *Val de Loire* and *Bretagne* during the winter on the Poole-Santander route. *(John Bryant)*

Above: The *Condor Express* seen outward-bound for Guernsey at the Sandbanks in May 1997. The impressive fast craft has had mixed fortunes on the Channel Islands routes. *(John May)*

Below: The *Bretagne* is seen here leaving St. Malo on her nine hour passage to Portsmouth. The St. Malo operation for Brittany Ferries has been the 'jewel in the crown' of their operations since the *Bretagne's* transfer to the route in 1993. This view also takes in a Trident class vessel of Emeraude Lines arriving at the Breton port from Jersey. *(Miles Cowsill)*

Above: Built as the **Nils Holgersson** for TT Line for the Travemunde-Trelleborg route. In 1991 she was purchased by Brittany Ferries and converted in Italy for the Plymouth-Santander route and Roscoff-Plymouth-Cork service. She has also operated on the Caen-Portsmouth route during the winter period for the company. She is seen here outward-bound for Roscoff in August 1993. *(Miles Cowsill)*

Below: Very much the grand lady of the Brittany Ferries' fleet, the **Quiberon** is seen here leaving Plymouth for her home port of Roscoff. Originally built as the **Nils Dacke**, the vessel was purchased by Brittany Ferries in 1984 and has been valuable tonnage for the company operating to date on all their routes apart from Cherbourg. *(Matthew Punter)*

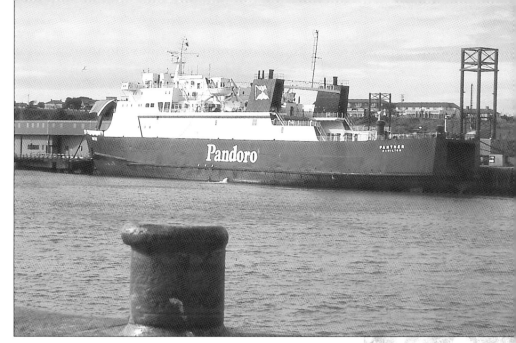

Above: Built as the **European Clearway** for Townsend Thoresen, she was later sold to Pandoro Ferries in 1993 to inaugurate their new Cherbourg-Rosslare service. The vessel was subsequently renamed **Panther** in 1996. She is seen here at Rosslare following her early morning arrival from Cherbourg in July 1997. *(Miles Cowsill)*

Below: Red Funnel Ferries introduced three new car ferries on their Southampton-Cowes service in the nineties. The first two vessels, the **Red Falcon** (pictured here) and the **Red Osprey** entered service in 1994; the third sister, the **Red Eagle,** was introduced some two years' later. *(FotoFlite)*

The *Stena Fantasia* and *SuperSeaCat Two* seen in Dover Strait in August 1997. *(FotoFlite)*

Above: Wightlink currently operate two ferry services from the mainland to the Isle of Wight. Their premier route is the Portsmouth-Fishbourne service which is operated by four near-identical ships: the *St. Catherine*, *St. Helen*, *St. Cecilia* and the newest of them the *St. Faith*, pictured here leaving Portsmouth in August 1997. *(Miles Cowsill)*

Below: The *Solidor 3* seen arriving at Jersey in her first season on the St. Malo-St. Helier service. The Norwegian-built vessel has proved a very reliable craft for the French company, following the disastrous operations of the earlier fast craft *Emeraude* in 1994. *(Dave Hocquard)*

The Portsmouth-Guernsey and Jersey freight services are currently maintained by Commodore Ferries. Two newly-constructed vessels the *Island Commodore* and *Commodore Goodwill* (pictured here) operate the twice-daily service from each port for the Guernsey based company. Both Dutch-built ships have a service speed of 18.3 knots and a passenger capacity for twelve drivers. *(Miles Cowsill)*

Chapter 2

Above: The *Olau Hollandia* seen at Bremerhaven undergoing her annual overhaul in 1993. Olau's operations between Sheerness and Vlissingen ceased in May 1994. Both the *Olau Hollandia* and *Olau Britannia* were then chartered to P&O European Ferries. *(Mike Louagie)*

Page 33 Top Picture: Following the demise of Olau Line, a freight service was started up by Ferrylink using two Egyptian vessels, the *Al Hussein* and *Nuwayba*. (pictured above right) Ferrylink changed their identity in January 1995 to Eurolink Ferries and introduced two new ships in March 1995, using two chartered Greek vessels by the name of *Euromagique* and *Euromantique* (pictured below right). The company's operations were only short-lived due to both vessels' unsuitability and lack of good accommodation compared to the former Olau operation. Eurolink's service closed on 1st December 1996. *(FotoFlite)*

Above: The small Euro-class vessels *European Trader, European Clearway* and *European Endeavour* have been transferred from the Dover Strait to the Irish Sea during the last five years. The 'Trader' and the 'Endeavour' currently operate between Larne and Cairnryan, while the *European Clearway* now renamed *Panther* operates for Pandoro - See page 27. The *European Endeavour* is seen here inward to Dover in a westerly gale. *(Mike Louagie)*

Below: The much-travelled French-registered *Chartres* is seen here leaving the Vandamme Lock at Zeebrugge in June 1990 in ALA livery. The *Chartres* completed her last season on the Dover Strait in 1993 and was subsequently sold to Greece for further service. Today she operates as the *Express Santorini*. *(Mike Louagie)*

The traditional car ferries **Sally Sky** and **Sally Star** were withdrawn from the Ramsgate-Dunkerque West route in 1997 in the light of reorganisation of the company and also increased competition on the Dover-Calais route. The top view shows, the **Sally Sky** arriving at Dunkerque escorted by the pilot. The view below shows, the **Sally Star** is seen outward-bound from the French port in her original livery. *(Mike Louagie)*

The series of eight Free Enterprise class ships were much admired by other operators on the English Channel. Today only one of the vessels still operates in British waters, the **Pride of Rathlin** (ex. **Pride of Walmer**, ex. **Free Enterprise VII**). Following the closure of the Dover-Boulogne route in 1993, the **Pride of Canterbury** (pictured below) and the **Pride of Hythe** were sold. The jumboised vessels **Pride of Walmer** and **Pride of Sandwich** (pictured above) maintained the Zeebrugge route until 1994, when they were subsequently both transferred to the Larne-Cairnryan route. *(Mike Louagie)*

Above: In 1995 P&O European Ferries decided to close their Felixstowe-Zeebrugge passenger service. The *Pride of Flanders* and *Pride of Suffolk* were subsequently converted back to freight ships for their new role on the Felixstowe-Europoort service. *(Mike Louagie)*

Below: A sad day in Belgian merchant history. The *Prins Filip* is seen here arriving at Ramsgate for the last time on 28th February 1997. *(Miles Cowsill)*

Following Sealink Stena Line's withdrawal from the Folkestone-Boulogne service, Opale Ferries inaugurated a freight-only service in 1992 using the *Marine Evangeline*. In 1993 the company went into liquidation and the service and the charter of the Canadian vessel were taken over by Meridian Ferries. The *Marine Evangeline* was subsequently renamed *Spirit of Boulogne* (pictured above). Later the company chartered from Corsica Ferries the former B&I vessel *Innisfallen* to support the operations. The former Irish vessel was renamed *Spirit of Independence* (pictured below) for her new role which was to prove unsuccessful with the company's demise later in March 1995. *(Miles Cowsill/FotoFlite)*

Above: With the demand for additional capacity on the Newhaven-Dieppe service, Stena Sealink Line chartered the *Vinzia E* (ex. *Wesertal*) in 1993. The chartered ship is seen here arriving at Dieppe during her first season on the link. *(Miles Cowsill)*

Below: Stena Line introduced their fast ferry service on the Newhaven-Dieppe route in 1996 using the *Stena Pegasus*. A series of mechanical and technical problems plagued the Italian-built craft She was subsequently withdrawn and later replaced by the *Stena Lynx III*. The attractive mono-hulled craft is seen here arriving at Newhaven in the late evening sun from Dieppe in August 1996. *(Miles Cowsill)*

The attractive-looking **Armorique** laid up at St. Malo prior to her sale to China. The **Armorique** was the mainstay of Brittany Ferries' operations for over 18 years. *(Miles Cowsill)*

Above: The former B&I vessel *Connacht* was purchased by Brittany Ferries in 1988 for the St. Malo route. She was subsequently sold eight years' later for further use in the Adriatic. The *Duchesse Anne* is seen here arriving at Portsmouth from St. Malo in May 1989. *(Miles Cowsill)*

Below: The *Beauport* (ex. *Reine Mathilde*, ex. *Prince of Brittany*, ex. *Prince of Fundy*) is seen here arriving at St. Peter Port in the last year of operation of British Channel Island Ferries. BCIF ceased trading in 1994 when Condor Ferries took over the Channel Island services. *(Miles Cowsill)*

Top - Page 42: The *Stena Normandy* opened the Southampton-Cherbourg service in 1991. Increased competition from the Channel Tunnel and the established services from Portsmouth were to see the demise of the operation five years' later. After a short spell in the Baltic in 1997, the vessel is due to return to the English Channel in 1998, to operate for Irish Ferries. *(FotoFlite)*

Middle - Page 42: Due to increased competition on the Dover Strait, the *Normandie Shipper* was withdrawn from service by Brittany Ferries in 1996 from the Caen-Portsmouth route. The vessel is seen here passing the *Barfleur* whilst operating on the Cherbourg-Poole service in 1993. *(FotoFlite)*

Bottom - Page 42: Following the introduction of the *Red Eagle*, the *Netley Castle* was withdrawn from service after 22 years of service on the Solent. *(Miles Cowsill)*

Above: The *Pride of Bilbao* seen on her maiden voyage to Bilbao in April 1993. *(FotoFlite)*

Two views of the *Prins Filip* seen under construction at Temse in March 1991. The new Belgian 'superferry' entered service in May 1992 on the Ostend-Dover link. The introduction of the vessel should have seen better fortunes for the Belgian company but sadly the demise of the company and its fleet were only five years away. *(Miles Cowsill)*

This wonderful view taken by FotoFlite shows the graceful *Princesse Astrid* on passage to Dover in her original livery of black hull, white superstructure and yellow & black funnel. *(FotoFlite)*

Above: RMT chartered the **Stena Nordica** (ex. **Stena Danica**) in May 1983. The ship was ideal for the increased freight capacity required as she had been jumboised in 1977 to offer an additional upper freight deck. In 1984, the vessel was renamed **Stena Nautica**. She remained on charter to RMT until 1986 when she was purchased by SNCF for the Newhaven-Dieppe route. *(Mike Louagie)*

Below: The growing need for even more freight space on the Ostend route prompted the company to initially charter the **Stena Nautica** from Stena Line. Although very slow for the route, she was the answer with a freight capacity for 43 units. The ship was purchased in February 1983 and later named **Reine Astrid**. She is seen here arriving at Ostend as the **Reine Astrid**. *(Mike Louagie)*

Above: In 1985, RMT announced that the **Prinses Maria-Esmeralda** and the **Princesse Marie-Christine** would be jumboised, cutting the ships horizontally and inserting an additional lorry deck, increasing their capacity from 46 to 55 trailers. The 'PMC' is seen here arriving at Ostend prior to her jumboisation. *(Mike Louagie)*

Below: In May 1981, RMT introduced a new 100 minute service between the ports of Ostend and Dover, using the Jetfoil craft **Princesse Clementine** and the **Prinses Stephanie**. The service proved popular, but expensive to operate for the Belgian company. The 'Clementine' is seen here off Ostend inward bound. *(Mike Louagie)*

In January 1986, RMT ended their joint operating agreement with Sealink (UK) Limited. They joined forces with Townsend Thoresen in a joint marketing operation. The **Princesse Clementine** (pictured above) is seen at the jetfoil berth at Ostend sporting the Townsend Thoresen livery while the **Prinses Paola** is seen in the new livery in gale force 10 conditions inward-bound to her home port. *(Miles Cowsill)*

RMT decided to end their marketing agreement with Townsend Thoresen in 1990. A new livery was adopted by the company of dark blue and pale blue hull with matching funnel. The *Reine Astrid* is seen here arriving at Ostend sporting the new livery and image of the company. *(Mike Louagie)*

Above: This view shows the **Princesse Marie-Christine**, after her jumboisation in the blue livery adopted by the company in the early nineties. This view clearly shows the additional freight deck and the sponsons on the side of the hull to take the extra accommodation. *(Mike Louagie)*

Below: Prior to the entry of the **Prins Filip** into service, the RMT fleet were repainted in yet another new livery of the Dover-Ostend Line. The **Princesse Marie-Christine** is seen here leaving Ostend for Dover in a winter gale. *(Mike Louagie)*

Above: The *Prince Laurent* seen arriving at Ostend was sold by RMT in 1992. Today she operates as the *Superferry II*. *(Mike Louagie)*

Below: The *Prins Albert* leaves Ostend in a strong easterly gale. This vessel was jumboised in January 1986. *(Mike Louagie)*

The **Princesse Clementine** on her annual overhaul at Ostend. *(Mike Louagie)*

Above: The *Prinses Stephanie* sweeps into Ostend harbour on her 100 minute dash from Dover on her last season operating from the Kentish port. *(Mike Louagie)*

Below: The *Pride of Dover* and the *Prins Filip* seen at Eastern Docks, Dover. The *Prins Filip* closed the Dover link on 31st December 1993 in favour of Ramsgate as their UK port. The company with their move to Ramsgate joined Sally Ferries in a joint marketing campaign. *(Mike Louagie)*

Above: The *Princesse Marie-Christine* arriving at Ostend sporting the Ostend Line's livery. *(Mike Louagie)*

Below: This aerial view of Ostend harbour shows the *Princesse Marie-Christine* bow in at the linkspan pending her afternoon departure to Ramsgate. *(Mike Louagie)*

Above: The redundant Jetfoils *Princesse Clementine* and *Prinses Stephanie* laid up at Ostend in October 1997 awaiting their fate. *(Miles Cowsill)*

Below: Following the demise of Ostend Line, the three conventional ferries were sent to Dunkerque for lay-up and sale. This view shows the *Prins Filip* in the evening sunlight at the French port laid-up for sale. *(John May)*

Further reading on the English Channel from Ferry Publications

Stena Line - The Fleet A comprehensive review of the fleet of Stena Line in full colour. A5, 40 pages. The book charts the history of Stena Line and includes detailed statistical information on each vessel in the fleet with picture. Price £5.50 inc p&p.

Ferries of the British Isles & Northern Europe 1997 Expanded and improved edition of this authoritative book, giving fleet operations of the British Isles and Northern Europe. A5, 168 pages. Price inc p&p £9.30

Ferry Port Dover The development of cross Channel vehicle ferries, their services and allied infrastructure at the UK's premier ferry port. Limited edition, illustrated, edition of John Hendy's 40,000 word university thesis. A4, 128 pages. Price inc p&p £12 (Overseas £13)

Folkestone-Boulogne 1843-1991 Published in 1987, this book was updated to coincide with the route's premature closure on 31st December 1991. A5 format, 40 pages. Price inc p&p £3.60.

Newhaven-Dieppe - The Car Ferry Era The book briefly traces the early days of the service until the introduction of the *Falaise* which opened the car ferry link in 1964. A detailed account follows her introduction up to the present day. A5, 56 pages, 8 pages of colour. Price inc p&p £4.70.

Ferries of Dover With the Channel Tunnel now open, the ferry companies at Dover have geared themselves up to counter the new fixed link. Includes a detailed account of the rise of the vehicle ferry through its 65 year history. Detailed fleet lists of past and present vessels. A5, with 8 pages of colour and over 80 black and white photos. Price inc p&p £5.95.

Ferries of Portsmouth & The Solent This 128 page, A5 book covers the history and development of Portsmouth Harbour since 1976. The title also includes a look at the Isle of Wight ferry services and other Solent operations. Detailed fleet list. 128 pages, of which 32 pages are in colour. Price inc p&p £8.20.

Ferries of the Channel Islands - Past and Present This book contains many outstanding pictures of the ferries which have plied the waters between mainland Britain and the Channel Islands. The book also includes a lot of the inter-island ferries and those vessels which have served with France. 56 pages. Price inc p&p £4.70.

The Dover-Ostend Line This A4, 56 paged publication traces the history of the historic route from its inception in 1846 until the building of the line's first super-ferry, the *Prins Filip*. With the transfer of the line to Ramsgate in 1994, this title will not be reprinted. Price inc p&p £7.10.

The Sealink Years This profusely illustrated book charts the story of the fleet, ports and routes from 1970 through to 1995, Published as a tribute to the ferry company whose name has for so long been synonymous with short sea travel around our coasts. 120 pages. Limited hardback copies £18.90 inc p&p, softback price £11.00 inc p&p.

ALL EUROPEAN & OVERSEAS ORDERS PLEASE ADD 85p
per order (unless stated otherwise)
Send cheque/postal order to
Ferry Publications, PO Box 9, Narberth,
Pembrokeshire, SA68 0YT.
Tel: +44 (0) 1834 891460 Fax: +44 (0) 1834 891463

John Bryant